# Brindled Words

Also by Antony Fawcus and published by Ginninderra Press
*Storms* (Pocket Poets)
*The Ethiopian Afar*
*Written in Sand*
*Gallimaufry*
*Midnight Echoes* (Pocket Poets)

**Antony Fawcus**

# Brindled Words

These poems are dedicated my late uncle, Henry Stokes,
the inspiration for 'Blackberrying'

*Brindled Words*
ISBN 978 1 76041 656 0
Copyright © Antony Fawcus 2018

First published 2018 by
**Ginninderra Press**
PO Box 3461 Port Adelaide 5015 Australia
www.ginninderrapress.com.au

# Contents

| | |
|---|---|
| Brindled Words | 9 |
| Leprechauns | 11 |
| Echo and Narcissus | 12 |
| The Kettle Boils | 13 |
| Butterfly Kisses | 14 |
| Blackberrying | 16 |
| Bess | 18 |
| The Blackbird is Flown | 20 |
| A Shattered Dream | 21 |
| Seeds of Hope | 22 |
| First Words | 23 |
| The Frogs | 24 |
| To Creativity | 25 |
| The Light Within | 26 |
| Bookend Ducks | 27 |
| Mooning | 28 |
| Out of Wedlock | 29 |
| A Need for Love | 30 |
| Deep in Thought | 31 |
| Dandelion Time | 32 |
| Huginn and Muninn | 33 |
| On Staffa | 34 |
| Puddles | 38 |
| Lunacy | 39 |
| The Blue Hare | 40 |
| Planting Seeds | 41 |
| Slack-jawed Tide | 42 |
| Mushroom Circles | 43 |
| Beneath the Surface | 44 |
| Rainmaker | 45 |

| | |
|---|---|
| Unknowns | 46 |
| Cockatoo | 47 |
| Bushfire | 48 |
| Hawk Moths | 49 |
| Northern Lights | 50 |
| Revenge | 51 |
| Repressed Emotions | 55 |
| Retribution | 56 |
| Water Carts | 59 |
| The Phoenix | 60 |
| Swarming Warning | 61 |
| A Ballad for the Duke of Orleans | 62 |
| The Tree | 63 |
| The Daffodil | 65 |
| The Fugitive | 66 |
| Dhara | 69 |
| Avalanche | 70 |
| A Dangerous Game | 72 |
| Rest in Peace | 74 |
| Forget Me Not | 75 |
| Keep Taking the Pills | 82 |
| When Life Runs Dry | 83 |
| A Summer Storm | 84 |
| The Gully Gully Man | 85 |
| Reaching In | 88 |
| Migration | 89 |
| The Tap Dancer | 91 |
| The Dandelion | 93 |
| Stained Glass | 95 |
| The Making of a Poem | 96 |
| Neruda | 98 |
| Hate | 99 |

| | |
|---|---|
| The Snowdrop | 100 |
| Yearning | 102 |
| Echoes of Eternity | 103 |
| Physical Maps | 105 |
| Ducks | 106 |
| Bigotry | 107 |
| A Reverie | 108 |
| Making Music | 109 |
| The Playground | 110 |
| The Moth | 111 |
| Freedom | 112 |
| Memento Mori | 114 |
| The Bees | 115 |
| Petrichor | 118 |
| The Refugee Children | 119 |
| The Goodnight Kiss | 121 |
| Faith | 122 |
| This is the Deep | 123 |
| A Pair of Piping Shrikes | 124 |
| Westminster Bridge, 22 March 2017 | 125 |
| The River | 126 |

# Brindled Words

Now shall I speak in brindled words
the brindled thoughts of poets wise,
whose scope of life and whim,
surmise and sighs,
and love for life,
is seen in ecstasies of weald and wood.

I hear their words on angels' wings
for, though these poets died,
their fears and loves survive,
transcending time
in harmonies that rise
to waft and wheel, then drop
with claws of steel
to pierce the soft of human stuff
and taffeta ordeal,
raising up such welts and weals
as resurrection deems it needs
to vanquish death.

My favoured book now falls,
its meld of life and rage consumed
in sleep, the blank of sheep
that will lamb anew
now all is still.
Diffuse the light of whispered dawn,
still damp with dew when I arise;
a no-man's-land, where lost souls scrawl
a half-scene purgatory of mists
that hang like flaccid sheets,

in the main awaiting
doldrum days, the listlessness
of lethargy and age,
until a gentle breeze
brings life again.

# Leprechauns

A *droighneach*

Leprechauns are hidden folk, fey and indistinct,
but not extinct, so don't believe their banes forbidden!
When they're chidden, their churlish tricks soon interlink
to cause a stink whose stench is worse than fish *ichthidin*!
So, if you feel forlorn, it's time to disengage.
When bearded men with eyes ablaze, hurl peppercorns
and winter storms, plan a pact and reappraise.
Strong poteen soon soothes the rage of little leprechauns!

# Echo and Narcissus

There lies a pool that holds my thoughts,
gouged out of rock, and veined with quartz,
whose crystal conduits distilled the
mirrored drops of purest silver;
reflections for
poor Narcissus
who did abhor
female kisses.
He did not wish to have a missus!
It was himself that he adored.

What fulfilment did he squander
when poor Echo drifted yonder?
What might have been? What might have been
if he had heard the violin?
If a dear wife
has the last word
throughout one's life,
she gets the bird.
I fear that he might have been stirred!
Trouble and strife! Beware the knife!

A narcissist
can get quite pissed.

# The Kettle Boils

A rondeau

The kettle boils and lets off steam –
enraged, I sometimes want to scream!
The neighbourhood can hear me roar
as I walk out and slam the door.
My patience lost, my ire's extreme.

Beware! My eyes will start to gleam –
a warning sign – a laser beam
that penetrates your very core.
The kettle boils!

But this is not what it might seem.
It's my own faults I would redeem.
It's with myself I'm feeling sore.
A cup of tea will soon restore
the balance of my self-esteem.
The kettle boils!

## Butterfly Kisses

Dear Teagan wore a pretty dress
adorned with butterflies.
When she reached in and pulled one out,
imagine my surprise!

The poor thing had till now been hid,
(Its true home was a tree)
but when she blew upon her hand,
she straightway set it free,

then very soon across the space
that she and Grandpa share,
more butterflies were blown abroad
like kisses in the air.

When the garden beds were filled
with wings that danced in space,
her cabbage whites' haphazard flight
had Grandma giving chase!

Her tortoiseshell transmogrified
into a purring cat!
She also freed fritillaries
to flit around my hat.

She then had Grandpa reaching in
to find *his* hidden store.
A mighty monarch spread its wings
and Teagan wanted more!

Although we now are worlds apart,
we have a hidden stash
that fly like dreams through cyberspace,

arriving in a flash!
Some days I have the chalk-hill blues
that waft like silent sighs,
but even when we're feeling sad,
we both have butterflies!

# Blackberrying

Today I stretched across the bramble years
to pick the luscious fruits of memory.
In doing so I caught my sleeve in briars;
the blood-stained sleeve on which my heart is worn.

Although the sun still shone and tiny birds,
cocksure with dainty step and beady eye,
played hide-and-seek with me about the bush,
my mind was lost in autumn reverie,
remembering the purple stain of times
when Henry led me down from Beaconcliff
with gloves and gaiters and with sickle blades
to slash a way through tangled undergrowth,
Death Valley bound, the source of Brownhill Creek.

We fiercely hacked a path, and backs were drenched
with sweat and insect swarms intent to sup,
until at last we reached a stand of trees,
whose Doric columns soared and took our eyes
beyond the canopy that held our dreams,
where filtered beams of light cut through the gloom
with hollow shafts suspending specks of gold,
and we were small in stillness, trapped in haze
of heavy scented eucalyptus leaves,
anointing all our sense with sacred oil.

Occasional elusive coloured birds
flashed through our line of sight, ephemeral,
still etched in mind long after they had gone,
as music lingers past the final note,
and then we heard the outrage of their screech,
their cry, 'Beware! Be gone, for strangers come!'

Our minds soon tuned into the insect whirr
and hum of bees that hovered on the flowers
in this our chapel, perilous and rare,
surrounded by a thicket hedge of thorns,
and mordant fruit beyond our wildest hopes.

We picked until the sun began to sink
then struggled back, bowed down with berry loads,
whose heavy press of juice dripped through the seams,
and when at last we reached our own domain
we poured the fruit in pots to make fresh jam
to give to friends, yet gifts we spread abroad
could not include the joy that we both felt,
for in these pickings we were sealing bonds
more firmly than the lids on jars of fruit,
a friendship now that's crystallised in words.

# Bess

Drowned moon, a dapple in the shallow mere
dispersed in swirling waves of vetchling grass,
as too the face of Bess, reflected there
and mocked among the weeds of this morass

where will-o-wisps mislead with eerie light,
where shadows merge at dusk with rising mist,
and blush of sea thrift pink is turned to white
as, chilled, she stumbles on to keep her tryst.

She hears ahead a groan of rusted iron
as on its hinges swings the kissing gate.
Beneath the glinting dagger of Orion
there stands the Essex lad who holds her fate.

He takes her in his arms, into the byre
where soon she lies spreadeagled, cruciform.
His whispered words of lust ignite her fire,
till ecstasy lights flames to keep her warm.

While in the Borrowdyke that lies beyond,
faint ripples break the surface of the night
as marsh frogs chortle softly in the pond,
locked in amplexus, each to each gripped tight.

As Bess and Ashe perform their puppet play,
they squirm, as do these frogs in seep and slime,
while Freyr pulls the strings of their affray
until they lose the very sense of time,

and in the shoreless firmament above
the changeling star of Betelgeuse looks on,
a silent witness to their dance of love
until the clouds are drawn and he is gone.

And did the red star frown when he gazed down
and did he think that love like this was wrong,
as did the men from nearby Chelmsford town
who burnt poor Bess before a gawking throng?

# The Blackbird is Flown

Though the blackbird is flown
and my hearing is gone,
I still hear the song,
its echo forlorn
in the jumble of years
amid atrophied layers
of my temporal lobe,
and the jumble of fears
as my heartstrings grow cold
and I journey alone…
I shall miss you, my dears.

# A Shattered Dream

Here, on the whale's back, a hump of hills
lies stretched along the coast, where Vulcan force
once shaped the writhing, molten land, now still
revered by generations past who dream
on Ngarrindjeri bones, ancestral songs
aligned with fractured seams, where they belong,

and here, each wintertime, the whales return,
slap-wallow tails and spurt their crystal spume,
to birth and tend the young leviathan
in shallow bays, but early settlers preyed
on them to fuel a want for light and hope
of scent and female corsetry – and soap

to wash away their sin. Thus the white men came
and, drenched in blood, they cut their homes from hills
along the coast, in savagery, and claimed
the stranded Dreamtime whale and made it yield
its fractured flesh to build their homes of stone,
embedding rights to call this land their own.

# Seeds of Hope

This is not my land. I do not belong.
If there's a way, I want to know,
how long?
Feel the gravid rocks; how slow

they are to birth the fragile soil,
and ask the man who husbands it
for livelihood, with toil,
unlike the lark that trills so sweet

with notes that greet the dawn.
How long have such birds sung?
Your song, too, is not forsworn
when you learn their tongue.

Listen, as a woodland wight
whispers up a sudden breeze,
then softly sing your inner light
into these gnarled, ill-fated trees.

Be still until, with inner eye
you sense the zephyr's soft caress,
as slow worms slither by,
tempting with the apple's kiss.

I'm but a stranger here
planting seeds of hope alone,
yet filled with awe, and fear
for this place that I'd call home.

# First Words

New words are still precious and rare
when you're two, so choose them with care!
Say 'More' when you want to explore,
'Enough' when the going gets tough.
'I do!' when you think that you might.
'Dada do!' if not going right!

When the sun shines, you say 'Outside!'
That's followed by 'Ride, Grandpa, ride!'
A piggyback down to the bed
with carrots in rows near the shed,
Now guess who the carrots are for!
A pony called Susie, for sure!

Say 'Carrot for Susie' – what fun!
as down to the paddock we run.
Dear Jenny is there with a rein.
'Ride, Susie!' again, and again.
'Enough, Teagan, now! Time for bed!'
brings out that word 'No!' that we dread!

# The Frogs

Deep in the depths of a concrete tank
(brekekekex ko-ax ko-ax)
the cacophonous chorus echoing sank
(brekekekex ko-ax ko-ax)
into the psyche of all around.
Crapulous chatter as revellers drank;
(brekekekex ko-ax ko-ax)

all night long no other sound,
(brekekekex ko-ax ko-ax)
scarcely coherent with regard to facts,
(brekekekex ko-ax ko-ax)
their minds in a muddle,
their brains rather lax,
(brekekekex ko-ax ko-ax)

How sad are these croaks
that maudlin folk make
when they wassail and wail
with Dionysian tales
of their sorrowful fate;
their woes and their gripes
brought out by the grape.

But what becomes of the drunks
that these froggies resemble
with their glassy eyes
and limbs all atremble,
so deeply sunk
in the Stygian lake
that there's no escape?

Charon awaits, his obol to take.

# To Creativity

Blank verse

What service do we to our gods when cast
in human mould, imagined small as man?
I would engender, gender free, a form
ineffable, amorphous, resonant,
and measureless, contained in all that is,
with some small fragment lodged in every life;
a spark enthused – *en theos* in the Greek –
with an immortal gift: creativeness.

How dull to merely live when we can shape,
as our maker did – and still does, in part
through us – an ever-growing universe
where every atom seeks its restless place;
where, in their rearrangement, words can say
fresh things, wrought in the furnace of our minds
and given life, as when the iron glows
from dormancy, to form the sword of truth.

How dull to merely live when we can be
creators of new life drawn from the source
of universal cognisance that dwells
deep down, within the reach of those who dare
to reach within. There is, beyond all darkness,
a blinding luminance that, if we choose,
is ours to share, a gift of life and love;
a godliness, through us made manifest.

# The Light Within

In the depths of the night the dreamer wakes
to himself, the co-creator,
whose light sears from the soul
to fire the clay,
to make strong the container
that holds the honeyed words of the gods,
a shared libation,
a draught to fan the flames,
disruptively erupting
with lava flow
to bury the artefacts of Pompeii,
the pompous artifices of Mammon,
and the household gods
of those blinded,
both by and from
the light that shines from within.
Dwell not upon it, dreamer,
lest your sight becomes shrivelled
in fear of its power,
but shield it boldly
to show you the way.

# Bookend Ducks

A sonnet

They stood like bookend ducks, alone, aloof.
Between them, dusty tomes of scholarship
that filled their minds with what they thought was truth;
a desiccated life, emotion stripped.

Their views researched and backed by ancient books,
their lust for life, in time, was oxidised;
a patina concealed their brazen looks,
as love became a thing hypothesised.

But what if they were buffed to make them glow,
and inward turned so, beak to beak, they kissed?
Would then they know themselves? Would their love grow,
and could they then retrieve what they had missed?

Though books may teach us much, our heart's the crux;
there is a deal to learn from loving ducks!

# Mooning

I am the man in the moon.
I feel the sun
upon my bum
and that's a boon.
My butt glows
in every phase,
for twenty-eight days.
So the whole world knows
I belong to a better class,
…the sun shines out of my arse.

# Out of Wedlock

A quatern

Her arm's outstretched, her fingers, too.
The one, once loved, is bound for hell;
she's drifting down… Is this farewell?
The days grow dark, and hopes are few.

The sun's last rays illuminate
her arm…outstretched. Her fingers, to
sweet wantonness must bid adieu,
and weakly wave, accepting fate.

She tasted of forbidden bliss
and must endure confinement's rue.
Her arm's outstretched, her fingers, too,
still hoping that, with tender kiss,

the bastard's father will renew
the hollow promise made last spring,
on bended knee, with wedding ring.
Her arm's outstretched…her finger, too.

# A Need for Love

A villanelle

Some days, the world is all too much to bear;
a monstrous banshee wails and thunders by,
and I have need of love to calm my fear…

a simple hug that shows me that you care,
a kiss to bring me comfort when I cry.
Some days, the world is all too much to bear.

I long to feel your fingers stroke my hair,
for now my sense of self is none too high,
and I have need of love to calm my fear.

I love the city's razzmatazz and glare,
but there are also times that terrify.
Some days, the world is…all too much to bear!

I can be brave. I know I can. So there!
But sometimes I am not, although I try,
and I have need of love to calm my fear.

In time, I'll meet with those who only jeer,
despising any weakness that they spy,
and, when the world becomes too much to bear,
I'll need your love again, to calm my fear.

# Deep in Thought

A rondelet

Much thought is due
before I gain the words to speak.
Much thought is due
in times like this while words accrue.
Each day I learn of life's mystique;
fresh marvels that unfold each week.
Much thought is due.

# Dandelion Time

Farewell, fly well, my parachutes
like spindrift spume, wind blown
from inkhorn seas and prancing waves
of words, unpenned and flown,

that we may grow in memories
of sunshine in the grass
to brighten up a life that's new
and help small worries pass.

So cheer me with your yellow hue
that I shall rely on
as I set sail on life's rough sea,
little dandelion!

# Huginn and Muninn

I knew two ravens; one was memory.
When I was young, he whispered in my ear;
he filled my mind with all there was to see,
and I went forth, devoid of any fear.

I knew it all, and with that knowledge, built
a citadel of great magnificence
upon the bones of others, without guilt,
whilst barely understanding my offence.

When wisdom came, he cocked his wise old head
and settled on my shoulder with a caw
that raised a spectral phalanx of the dead,
which should have brought my conscience to the fore,

but I was old, my memory had flown,
and I could not recall what I had sown.

# On Staffa

Within this cave of basalt rock,
cathedral columns rise,
hexagonal and steeply set,
beyond my wild surmise,

and echoes drift upon the wind
with notes of deep despair;
a Hebridean overture
inspired by soughing air,

its tones funereal and sad,
a dirge in minor key,
a bagpipe drone with dark bassoon,
and restless slop of sea.

There's a sad sweetness that exists
in Fingal's honeycomb,
whose hollow tones bewitched soft tunes
from Felix Mendelssohn.

With eagerness we scaled the rock,
aloft where steep stairs wind
above the gloom of shadowed past
as, breathlessly, we climbed

to heather brae and summer sky,
where paths, windswept and sparse,
were splashed with eyebright's lilac haze
of dots 'mid tussock grass.

Then down we sank to rest awhile,
while taking in the view
of sparkling mack'rel seas to Mull,
a distant, misty blue.

In time, we heard a throaty purr,
a buzzing scribble sound,
of puffins in their breeding dens,
well-hidden underground.

There soon emerged a rainbow beak
and small tuxedoed bird
that waddled by. She cocked an eye
– no doubt thought us absurd!

Then, off with whirring wing, she ran
the gauntlet of the skies.
Each time she makes this flight to fish,
this tiny auk defies

a flock of vicious black-backed gulls
that hover overhead.
A *danse macabre* starts, whose steps
fill tiny hearts with dread.

A lucky few win through, transformed,
no longer Harlequin,
but dancers now, with fluid grace,
that pirouette and spin,

each fish dive dance a graceful move,
with swift, adroit glissade.
At length, they breast the wave again,
with sand eel catch displayed

for gulls to snatch. The puffins skim
the surf and scurry home,
while skuas shriek and swoop to scrag
the stragglers, beak and bone.

We are transfixed as they evade
this maelstrom in the air,
and then, as sudden as she left,
our comic reappears

and scuttles to her burrow, safe,
so we again are blessed
with a maternal puffin purr
that signifies success.

We talk a while, considering
our sunny outcrop throne.
A giant with volcanic force
begot this stepping stone,

kin to the Giant's Causeway found
on Erin's northern shores,
whence Fingal sailed, in Celtic myth,
to fight in Viking wars,

as his son Ossian described
in James McPherson's tome,
his lance 'a meteor of death'
reflected in the moon.

And does the ghost of Fingal still
repel fierce Valkyries,
as down they swoop upon small birds
in basalt galleries?

As I recall this Staffa day,
the clock forbears to chime,
for when one sinks in reverie,
the self retires from time!

# Puddles

When all the world seems grey and dark,
and rain has swept across the park,
observe, with childlike innocence,
reflections of the trees and sky,
and how the clouds go flying by.
For children this is more intense.
Mere thought? No child would stop at that.
They jump right in! Both feet go splat!
When life's a game, it makes more sense.

## Lunacy

Bait your hook with words.
Lunacy?
Dreams can turn the tide.

# The Blue Hare

A sudden crystal dance,
in frost-sparked air,
where once you were,
electric blue and charged with fear.

An icy chill sets in,
as you fade into the mist,
immortal hare.

Your ghost still here,
the essence of this winter world.
Splintered shards of light
shake powdered snow from trees,
a host of little shivers;
joy to share.

## Planting Seeds

I shall rise to greet the dawn
on this fine day,
trusting that my heart will guide
my feet of clay.

I shall dig, and plant small seeds
in this rich soil
then, with patience, watch them grow,
and rest from toil

while the sun warms what I sowed
with loving care.
If dark clouds should fill the sky
and chill the air

I welcome them, for they bring
the gift of rain,
and I know that when they pass
there's sun again.

In this life both rain and shine
make wisdom grow,
so I shall plant seeds galore
before I go.

# Slack-jawed Tide

Silver still the sea tonight,
a luminescent, viscous thing
of listless lull,
and solipsistic slop
and murmuring,
that softly sucks the life from hidden holes
where monsters lurk and wild imaginings
drift dead men in to shore
on slack-jawed tides
and drag them out again,
where gormless hagfish swirl and swim
beneath the dark viridian
of clinging kelp and bottle-blue *physalia*,
whose lethal droop of tentacles
hangs low
to drift,
and sting.

# Mushroom Circles

Wild mushrooms damp with early morning dew
still hold the scent of dark seductive night,
pubescent ripeness shyly held from view,
pink round the gills, and satin skin stretched tight.

Beware all those who step within this ring,
their dormancy of dreams undone by dance,
for faerie folk weave magic here, to sing
their souls adrift, to captivate – entrance.

Let lambent leaves of oak shake off the shade,
let wind and withy spindles spin and sway.
But, in the faerie circle, all things fade.
All those who enter in are trapped by fey.

In webs of woven moonlight evermore,
all memories of bacchanal are gone,
the revelries they dreamt at witching hour,
in mocking echoes fail. The curtain's drawn.

# Beneath the Surface

How far behind those lips was born that half-formed smile?
Their parting holds a pledge, a door that's held ajar.
With hesitating heart, I wonder who it's for –
that enigmatic look that hovers, to beguile.

What strange imaginings of love, what treasures held
in caves beyond the petals of the damask rose
where nectar is, and heavy scents, delights for those
that part the moistened lips in bliss – at last – to meld.

How deep the flecks of green in those grey seas, the eyes
that dare the man bewitched, be bold to venture in,
to sport with dolphins, hear the song of whales, to swim,
perhaps to drown in time, in wild desires and sighs.

What oystered pearl, my Nereid, lies on your bed
amid the swirl and silver glint of shoals that pass,
as do the ripples of your silken gown, alas,
when, with disdain you flounce away, and cut me dead?

# Rainmaker

Beat on your drums like a thunder of hooves,
rouse me from slumber and the depths of my trance,
with your frenzy of feet aping rain on tin rooves,
for my magic responds to the rhythm of dance.

I'm a spinner of winds and conceiver of clouds,
cloaking the sapphire of sere summer days,
weaving confusion, a shadow that shrouds
Nature's vast space in mysterious ways.

Shaping sharp squalls, sullen with rain,
creating the madness and turmoil of storms;
deft with delusions to buffet the brain,
illusive electrics, bolts and alarms.

When drought has induced the depths of despair,
I can conjure up raindrops for pitiless thirst,
or call down a deluge from the energised air,
to douse raging fires with a sudden cloudburst.

So, beat on your drums and summon a song,
rouse me from slumber to practice my art,
mesmerise me with a rhythm that's strong,
for I am bewitched when you spellbind my heart.

# Unknowns

There is in life an x, unknown,
so let us call it God,
and let us solve our lives for x –
a postulate that's odd

when reason also looks for why,
another undefined,
a simultaneous mystery
Math'matics has divined,

but we can solve our lives for x
if logic is displaced,
by taking why right out of it,
and substituting faith.

# Cockatoo

doom black cockatoo
yellow tail
discordant screech-shrill flight
flocks wheel and flow
in motion, slow
with lazy flap
and raucous skirl
squabble, circle, whirl,
they settle now
rapacious feast
beak-torn
pine cone whorls
strewn below

# Bushfire

By noon the trees are peeling paperbark,
red ochre scars and pink new skin exposed;
oil, oozed from pores, hangs listless in the air,
as sweating eucalypts withstand the sun
as best they can. Beneath their scanty shade,
a herd of kine lies still, their roan and brown
a speckled camouflage in flaxen grass
that, brittle, waits a spark to animate
this sultry lassitude of summer heat,
whose haze of blue asphyxiates the bush,
where parrots gag for breath, and small birds shrink
into the shadowed wattle undergrowth.

A slight breeze stirs, to fan a whiff of smoke,
uprearing, like a snake, from near a shard
of glass, to feel the air with flickered tongue.
Then flame spills fast across the dried-out seed,
and crackles in a flurry, raw with fear.
The dragon breathes once more upon this earth,
to cleanse its ancient frame of burnished bones,
yet from the charred remains new growth will come,
for where there's life that still exists, there's hope.

## Hawk Moths

The air tonight's distilled from jasmine flowers,
a whiff of pheromone.
Hawk moths hover,
tipsy wraiths that waft from cup to cup,
with casual promiscuity,
till lifted by a sultry sigh
to kiss the sequined, velvet dress of night
on wings of moonlit lace.

# Northern Lights

Dissolved lights rise like spectral eyes
when Viking gods awake the sky's
haphazard glow. A writhing show
of rose and bruise begins to grow.

As forked tongues snake, their eerie wake
recalls brave men who've crossed the lake
of time; their pyre, a restless fire.
Illusions form a firefly choir

in flight, a symphony of light
to mystify a star-strewn night
of eldrich spells above the hell
of kraken deeps, where monsters dwell.

# Revenge

Wild fly their feathered tails as stallions stamp
and snort a trailing mist of billowed breath.
Their wide eyes gleam with fear, their flanks still damp
with dew condensed from skies foretelling death
as night subsides, to sleep in buried woods
beyond the glare, the joyless glare of day.
Behold, the riders come with glinting swords,
and spurs to goad these steeds in blinkered hoods,
that paw the brazen earth in fierce display,
and neigh at the approach of their grim lords.

Amid the turbulence of stamping hooves
was one who stood in stirrups, tall and fair,
surveying smouldered peat of peasant rooves
and fields of golden corn now razed and bare,
and woodland ways, enjoyed in solitude
before that tragic day, when her horse shied
at sudden swoop and tumble-feathered claw
that ripped a rabbit's heart, its entrails strewed,
surprised by sudden force as all hope died…
the same she found when she rode home once more.

Her flowing locks were hid, her breastplate tight
constraining secret fires, catlike and lithe,
and, in her hectic eye, the hollow sight
of one who had been cut by death's sharp scythe
that swept across the land she once called home,
and severed from her bosom all her kin.
Her noble heart still heard the blood-wrenched screams
as those she loved were slain, and she alone
escaped by dint of fate, whose mocking grin
now drove her to fulfil tormented dreams.

Revenge was in her heart, a worm that grows
in scale when fanned from embers of dull hate,
unfurling shadowed wings on all her foes,
and claws, with venom spiked, to seal their fate.
For circumstance had turned this gentle lass
into a dragon queen, whose flames consumed
all those who crossed her paths of ashen grief.
She turned fresh fields of spring to withered grass
just as her foes had done when she was doomed,
and thus she shed her youth and her belief,

or so it seemed, as she upstaged the throng
to urge them on. 'Who rides with me?' she cried.
All growled assent in voices loud and strong,
save one sole nobleman whose voice replied
with gentleness and calm. He shook his head.
'Enough,' he said. Just then, a skylark rose,
with overflowing song, to greet the morn.
'See there, that bird, her song a silver thread
'of sorrow, spreading like a salve that flows
'to soothe away her grief…her nest is gone.

'Although forlorn, she'll build another soon.
'Her life goes on.' With that, he turned away
but, as he left, the echo of her tune
still drifted on the wind to bid him stay.
It's hard to tell who cast the stone or made
the coward call. A mob is of one voice,
and men of peace are often crucified.
Slow, he walked away, hurt but unafraid.
She freely let him go, the ghost of choice;
redemption offered, but the chance denied.

Determined to avenge herself in gore
on those who wrecked her home, her love, her life,
her spur dug in. She led her troop to war,
her chance to change foresworn for further strife.
Yet, for a time, she seemed preoccupied,
as she recalled the peace of former times
with hesitating mind, but still she fought
against a foe who gnawed at her, inside,
as visions flooded back of leprous crimes
and ate her heart, consuming every thought.

When loaded with the dross of anger, hate,
and bile, the scale weighs heavily in mind.
It takes an age to mine the counterweight;
forgiveness is a gem that's hard to find.
The fair maid's fate, in leaden casket sealed,
was thus assured as from the clear blue sky
a falcon flew across the barren heath,
unerringly towards the new-ploughed field
where last the lark's soft trill became a sigh,
and Cadmus sowed the fateful dragon's teeth.

# Repressed Emotions

I canter towards the dark; then come lamely home again.
These forays are all false starts; my intentions are in vain,
I'm led headlong by a heart that's perverted by my brain,
though virgin ground is tempting, I shall never leave a stain.

My life is bound by caution, I would toss it to the wind,
with hesitating footsteps, I have sometimes almost sinned.
Restrained by learnt convention, I am like an insect pinned,
a museum specimen, become frail and brittle-skinned.

Yet still there lurks a notion, when I view dark stars that gleam;
beyond childhood repression, subliminal cravings seem
to erect realities – no longer constrained by dream.
How the joys of life do melt. Mr Whippy rings. I scream.

# Retribution

Here chimes the bell, well amplified.
Its hollow tones reverberate
with echoed notes whose wraiths subside
in deathly chill. It summons late
inquisitors, whose shadows grow
grotesque on lamplit banks of snow
that flank the silent monuments
of long departed souls, from whence
the eerie twilight shadows moan
with sighs that mock the impudence
of one who thought The Path his own.

His silhouette and even stride
suggest a nobleman's estate;
a lord who would not be defied
by any man, or God, or Fate.
But hear the mighty trumpets blow,
collapsing walls of Jericho.
This evil man spares no expense
for pride, a failing so immense
it permeates his every bone,
sets him apart, the sole defence
of one who thought The Path his own.

He wielded rank and few denied
his whole demeanour made him grate,
a homophone that pricked his side,
this self-inflated potentate,
whose potency was hollow show
when judgement came to bring him low,
despite his barricade, a fence
surrounding years of falseness, hence
a gilded cage now turned to stone,
a heavy weight that dulls the sense
of one who thought The Path his own.

Upon this night the Fates decide
his doom. Their cunning thrusts deflate
his puffed up armament of pride.
There's nothing left to contemplate.
The verdict's read with solemn woe
like sombre organ notes that blow
by blow, condemn his dissidence.
He takes the stand, the air grows tense,
the judge decrees his life on loan
and strips away the last pretence
of one who thought the Path his own.

They challenged him and found he lied
when spreading words of wilful hate.
They opened up a chasm wide
to swallow him upon this date
that's etched with retribution's glow,
decreeing that he must forego
this life on earth, as they dispense
the punishment for his offence,
the stench of which, this tale has shown,
still rises like the foul incense
of one who thought the Path his own.

How judge you now this recompense?
The tyrant thought all others dense,
and took his place, with pride, alone,
and was condemned. Fair consequence
for one who thought the Path his own?

# Water Carts

Thus turns the wheel of life; a round
fulfilling needs and quenching thirst,
yet onerous, as women found –
six times a day. Each step was cursed

between the hut and riverside.
Thus turns the wheel of life, a round
to bend the stoutest back, each stride
traversed with care. Uneven ground,

where traps for weary feet abound,
miscarried those who were with child.
Thus turns the wheel of life around.
But, recently, good fortune smiled

when water carts were introduced;
a change with outcomes so profound
that even men are now seduced
to turn the wheel of life around!

# The Phoenix

Deep in the glowing embers I would seek
the fabled Phoenix, lost in ashen sleep.
Into his dormant dreams mine own would seep,
to reignite his fire and fan the flame.
Then, on his wing, I'd fly to heights unknown,
unleashing ancient words of potent worth
to spread his elder magic through the Earth;
uniting with his vision, to reclaim
those times when genteel knights, of erstwhile fame,
defended with their honour what is right
and vanquished monstrous evils in fair fight,
restoring to the kingdom honour's name.
With fiery zeal we'd resurrect the lore
to help this world redeem its peace once more.

# Swarming Warning

There is a buzzing in that tree –
a mighty bombination.
When the bees bear down on me,
the discombobulation
is a fundamental fear,
but baseless consternation!

A swarm that's from my apiary
should make me feel elation,
for they are chasing the queen bee –
not me – for copulation,
unless one bee has squarely
picked…a different destination!

# A Ballad for the Duke of Orleans

Good duke, I served against your foe
and now I stand before your gate,
a soldier whose portfolio
of verse extols your great estate.
I've travelled far, the hour is late,
I beg your leave, let me dismount in
immodest haste to bibulate.
I die of thirst beside the fountain!

To bibulate? If such words flow
like angry bees that bombinate,
my favours I will not bestow.
Such windbag words can only grate
on genteel minds, so clearly state
'imbibe' or 'drink!' You'll not be countin'
on gifts from me! I'll not debate –
so die of thirst beside the fountain!

Good duke, your boundless mercy show,
and I will modify my prate,
for I would drink to ease my woe.
I wish your foes could amputate
my lengthy words, but they castrate
the likes of me upon the mountain.
Now I shall perish, intestate.
I die of thirst beside the fountain.

Because Your Grace, by your dictate,
discovered nothing of account in
my turgid verse to adulate,
I die of thirst beside the fountain.

## The Tree

The tree at my front gate
I'd given up for dead,
gnarled joints and sere,
some straggle leaves below,
a last hurrah I thought,
and that was fifteen years,
or more,
ago.

Flocks of cockatoos sometimes come,
and settle on
its outstretched arms.
Their clamour mocks with raucous life
its long dead limbs,
while down below,
the straggle leaves gain strength and grow.

Its yearning limbs, on one wild night,
closed round a hunter's moon,
clasped its bulbous bloat,
in heartless mockery of life
but, rooted firm, could not take flight
like seas receding – tide untied –
for still its pendules stayed alive.

At dusk a whispered silhouette
posed against the charcoal sky,
a silent swoop, a sudden cry,
yet still the struggle leaves possessed
their pulsing thread of sap,
undaunted by the death throes of
such heart-torn prey.

I might have written off that tree,
but it still lives, tenaciously.
Old things surprise;
as, too, may I.

# The Daffodil

Into the flower's throat I fly,
a cave of anther'd gold,
and there I lie,
in my mind's eye,
to listen to her tale unfold.

Long days of solitude and dread,
waiting, waiting in the cold,
among the living dead,
in winter's bed,
covered by a leafy mould.

Then slowly comes a seeping thaw,
a dream of sunshine overhead,
a dream to warm her inner core,
until she pushes through the floor,
and shadowed whispers spread.

Wild with spring, her question mark uncurls,
exclaiming, 'Winter's done, new life is here!'
She joins a joyful host, her flag unfurls,
as off I fly again, to pollinate the world,
her March-blown trumpet yellowing the air.

# The Fugitive

O fugitive, from whom and whence your flight,
with trepid step and eye of mirrored fear,
that casts its nervous glance from left to right
as shadows shift like wraiths to mock the ear
and touch the tattered garment of your mind,
deranged by horrid whispers of the past;
dismembered times, when night's dull orbs were blind,
ashamed to shine and so, concealed, aghast,

in tear-stained shrouds? Each edge of silvered smear
shows where the evil things have slowly sprawled
across a seething ferment of despair
and leered, as one sadistic monster crawled
to squeeze the moon of fragile hopes possessed,
and drape them on the tumult of the sky
in sacrificial splendour, like those oppressed
below, in huddled groups, about to die.

O fugitive! Was that to be your due?
And how did you escape? Was it the sum
of motherhood that clasped and smothered you
within her shattered breast, and silenced thrum
of broken heart, and life that ebbed away?
And did that willing shield protect you still,
until the dying embers of the day
gave way to ash at last, and night time chill?

And did you crawl from under her dead weight
with only that small fragment from her dress
clutched to a heart, as yet not filled with hate,
but only with the anguish of distress,
and cold with shock? And did you wildly run,
and still run on, despite the burning breath
that seared your heaving chest, until the sun
came up again, once more defeating death?

Then, there ahead, the cleansing ocean lay,
an endless calm beneath the burnished mist
with seagulls clamouring to greet the day
while ripples lapped the shore and shyly kissed
the shining strand, and then fell back once more,
abashed, until the surge emboldened them
to toss small gifts of fragile shells ashore
and woo the sands again with sea sprite gems.

And did you swim to cleanse away the grime,
enchanted by Calypso's sun-flecked smiles,
as her dolphin pod, suspending time,
enticed your soul to seek the Blessèd Isles?
But you were saved it seems, and did not drown;
at least not yet. A simple fisherman
spied you among the flotsam weed, weighed down
and near to death. His wrinkled face, suntanned

and wreathed in smiles, regarded your limp form
that retched with life anew upon the floor,
wrapped in a homespun rug to keep you warm.
Then winds that bore the acrid stench of war
sprang up to drive you west towards a life
on foreign soil far from your home, exiled,
where you could start afresh, away from strife;
a refugee behind barbed wire, reviled

by those who live a life of ease, in fear
of desperate men displaced and dispossessed,
and little princelings too, like you, Amir;
orphaned, frightened souls, seeking love and rest.
And will you find compassion or blind hate
and prejudice; new terrors to brave out,
more subtle than those horrors borne of late?
Will trust forever be displaced by doubt?

O fugitive, from whom and whence your flight,
with trepid step and eye of mirrored fear,
that casts its nervous glance from left to right
as shadows shift like wraiths to mock the ear
and touch the tattered garment of your mind,
deranged by horrid whispers that persist,
to drive you mad? Are night's dull orbs still blind,
ashamed to shine, or can we co-exist?

## Dhara

Feel the strength, resilience and grace
in this fine face
that hardship's honed;
capable and dignified, as women are,
in the Afar.
She's not unique;
just one more
inspiring awe
in us.

## **Avalanche**

Snow lies on the hill,
sleep in the valley,
all now is calm;
and grey skies forlorn.

With methodical footsteps
I make for the chalet,
though the contour's erased,
blanked out by the storm.

Upwards and onward,
a trail of depressions,
each footprint won
from the steep mountain path,
defining my fore, and
aftermath,
impassively spun, as The Fates look on.

I intrude on the calm
and my presence alarms
a bird's wing, bestirred
from a snow-laden bough,
its whir and its flurry
clouding my eye
with a feathery fall,

then sudden cascade.

An ominous echo
runs down to the valley,
with a gathering rage
of pine trees and rock,
an avalanche launched
hurling death down the gully,

as the bird flies away
and I fall to my knees.

# A Dangerous Game

In better times
he was ensconced
in candelabra arms,
D cup at least,
(a silver-plated investment).

How came he to this guttered state
stuck in the neck of a bottle,
drained in gulps
of epiglottal snot
and snuffle,
to whine away his life
with cheap Rosé;

the love
she couldn't hold
a candle to,
or match?

O candle,
where is now your candlestick,
the one that held your flame
and waxen wick,
drip by drip,
to slowly wane?

He once waxed hot,
his flickered tongue inflamed
in matrimonial strife.
One breath, one blow;
a snuffed out
life.

Her glassy eye stared up at him
aghast,
and now the dregs in the bottle
haunt his mind
with this vision of
a throttled
axolotl.

It did not take the jury long
to reach their grim verdict,

that Colonel Mustard did it,
in the study,
with the candlestick.

# Rest in Peace

Be still,
I bid you; still
as the translucent stars
condensed from night's cold breath, my love,
adieu.

Adieu,
I bid you – still
as the dark stars I wept
to rest my love from night-cold air.
Be still.

# Forget Me Not

Roots curl around the moisture of cold stone,
when shy forget-me-nots, whom death deceive,
defy belief, as they take life on loan
in fissures, where, tenaciously, they cleave
to hope, despite their half-starved circumstance,
and still put forth their precious stars of blue.
Such plants push past the stone where, at first glance,
one might expect a life of paler hue.
Because the mortar's cracked, these steps sustain
a garden wilderness of displaced seed
that winds of chance have dropped, then fates ordain
their task, to bring to barrenness their creed,
by thrusting roots to dampness found below,
when summer heat beats down like molten gold.
For, with determination, all can grow,
despite the tenuous nature of their hold.
It's in adversity we often thrive
against the odds, intent to stay alive.

Against the odds, intent to stay alive,
this house, that's built of local quarried rock,
has stood the test of time, to still survive;
well-built to stand the ticking of the clock.
Its porch (alas, of wood!) is honeycombed
with rot; its rheumy eyes turn to the coast,
some panes, that creak and groan, at last succumb
to winds that haunt them, howling like a ghost.
They inwards fall, exposing yawning gaps
where birds come in to build their nests of straw
in long discarded hats, well lined with scraps
they scavenged from a half-forgotten store
of bric-a-brac, and there they raise their brood.
An east wind blows through gaps in broken tiles,
and rain now stains discarded things accrued,
consigned to 'may be useful sometime' piles.
Vague memories of better days live on,
like echoes, though their usefulness is gone.

Like echoes, though their usefulness is gone,
a set of clubs, used ninety years ago
by father, when his golfing prowess shone;
his niblick glints to catch the golden glow
as sunset casts its shadow on the past.
Then cold condenses drops of night-time dew,
old gutters weep their silent tears of rust,
and yellow eyes in hollows whisper, 'Who?'
When morning comes, the stone soaks up the sun,
and I ascend the steps to reach the door,
intent to renovate – a task begun
in mind, a year or two ago, before
the rats moved in and lined their ceiling nest
with warm alpaca fleece I meant to spin
but stored against some day to come, less stressed;
a fate that met my uncle's mandolin
that leans against a wall with silent noise,
untuned (as is my focus on such joys).

Untuned, as is my focus on such joys,
I look about, and wonder where to start.
My eyes light on a chest of childhood toys;
the ancient chest and toys both claim my heart.
So they, and almost all the rest, are stored
elsewhere while work begins. A soul resides
in most such things that we are apt to hoard;
a lifetime's worth of memories besides.
And so it is with this old porch, ingrained
with love. Its timbers came from early ships,
constructed with a craftsman's care and stained
with sweat. Though life was hard, they came to grips
and carved a home from local stone and wood,
with simple hand-held tools and joiners' arts
now seldom used, or taught, or understood.
I took good care; dismembered all the parts
with due regard for how to build again –
such lessons of the past are not arcane.

Such lessons of the past are not arcane,
for secrets locked in death are manifest
with careful observation, to unchain
the sequence, as the building is undressed.
But that undressing done, it's time to act,
with dovetailed love, ingrained, to give new life,
yet keep the soul of yesteryear intact,
with younger woods withstanding nature's strife.
At last the frame is up, built true and square.
New panes are pinned to muntins, puttied in.
The matchboard's painted bright, no longer bare!
The roof, like us, is galvanised, with tin-
tinnabulations ringing out, 'Rejoice!'
When rain pelts down, and I am safe inside,
with shelter from the elements – give voice!
The ocean's surge and swell's demystified
when through the pane, the swaying trees are seen
extending echoes of new life again;

extending echoes of new life again,
in peaceful rocking days where horses trot,
then gallop by, with urgency insane,
while old men dream their lives away and rot.
Perhaps, in years to come, when I am frail,
a kindly nurse will place my bed out here,
So I can see the sea before I fail.
Though mists obscure, a wider view is clear,
across the flower beds and greening lawn,
to stables, where the mare's about to foal,
and out to sea, now eventide and calm,
a yawning void where night's celestial pole,
reflects the crux of life, a Candlemas
of stars, fomenting universal birth,
a shattered ceiling, shards of broken glass,
a crystal goblet, dashed with godly mirth.
Upon this stoep, a table and two chairs;
an empty one and one that's filled with fears.

An empty one and one that's filled with fears?
Are these for phantom guests, forgotten ghosts
that hover over my declining years?
At length, the circle's closed; there's Death to host
and entertain. We share the good things spilt,
the random seeds of thought that grow and thrive
to soften sharper angles I have built
for sake of symmetry, to house my lives.
Kaleidoscoping nights merge into days
with time-lapse clouds that scud away; a grim
montage, a fleeting glimpse of life erased
no sooner than it's felt – a phantom limb.
When life is on the ebb and thoughts are blue,
and rheumy eyes detect a blur of Heaven,
I'll contemplate these years of richer hue,
forgetting not the smaller gifts we're given.
This precious life's on loan, and when it's done,
roots curl around the moisture of cold stone.

# Keep Taking the Pills

My days are counted in a plastic box,
neatly sectioned, Morning, Noon and Night,
in case I forget which is which.
They're marked Monday to Sunday
that I may live weakly,
tablet to tablet,
until, one day,
I, too, am
neatly
boxed.

# When Life Runs Dry

When life runs dry and feelings shrink,
there is a brook I know
with words of wisdom poets wrote,
in ages long ago.

I dip my ladle in and drink
till filled with joy anew,
and with that draught I am refreshed,
as with the morning dew.

When in that shimmering stream I seek
to free my thoughts from woe,
I find that life is only drained
if I let it be so.

# A Summer Storm

In the dark foreshadowing of doom,
I slumped with measured tread
past London monoliths that rose
dejectedly
towards a glowering sky;
my thoughts like lead,

when, suddenly,
the sky was torn apart with blinding force.

Thunderstruck, I pulled up short
and raised the collar on my coat.
The rain began,
small drops at first
that slapped and stung my face,
whipped up by wind
into a furious assault
that left me cleansed,
elated by the primal force,
and soaked,
no longer in self-pity
and slum-pervaded thought,

but in the glorious freshness,
steam on stone,
as the glistening sun came out again,
defiantly adorning streets in evanescent gold.

It takes, at times,
a sudden storm to wash away the grime
from city streets – and living.

# The Gully Gully Man

Abdul, father's *syce*,
shines our jet black car
and buffs the chrome.
Pristine, we soon appear,
Mother, the memsa'ab,
in slinky Thai silk sheath
and well-matched pearls,
Father, debonair.

Off to famous Raffles
for Sunday curry tiffin
in steamy Singapore.

Gin slings for the girls, and *stengahs* for the men
Talk and tittle-tattle beneath the punkah-wallah's fan.
Then, when tiffin's done,
the men drift to their den.
Memsa'ab, now unsteady,
takes me by the hand,
her perfume commingling
with the frangipani tree.
as we join the chatting crowd.

A harbour foghorn blares
and, right on cue,
I see a red, black-tasselled fez,
a long white robe,
a battered leather case,
an air of majesty.

'Here comes the Gully Gully man,'
the whisper runs around.
There's a ripple in the crowd
as he spreads his tattered cloth
makes his mocking bow,
and grins
with gold-capped teeth.

Transfixed by his piercing eye,
I blanch
as he approaches me,
sweeps off his fez
and plucks an egg from out
behind my ear
and drops it in.
He dons the hat again,
then turns and whips it off;
a day-old chick is balanced on his head.
I am aghast!
He lifts the case's lid and pops it in.

And so the tricks go on,
small boy entranced,
and clapping hands with glee.

At length he turns again with smiles,
and lifting up the lid,
withdraws a full-grown hen,
that, clucking, strays across the lawn
as he dips in once more
to find an egg,
new-laid and warm,
to put behind my ear again –
then suddenly it's gone!

# Reaching In

How calm the sense of inner being is
when thought dissolves and we become ourselves,
then presence comes and pause from daily strife.
Each breath's inhaled with thanks for precious air;
when life seems stacked against us, still we breathe.
When water's pure, we drink, and so we live –
such simple pleasures, as we concentrate
on whom we really are, and on the pulse
of life that underlies our meaning here on earth.

Life need not be constructed from our past,
the mindless babble of our minds and tongues.
In finding what's within when we reach down,
we draw upon the strength to make our mark,
set free from all the scars that life inflicts.

We're not the sum of such external wounds
imposed. Breathe deep and free your mind from thought,
the heavy weight that drags us from our craft
and causes us to drown, so cut the line.

Release the inner self and build anew,
from that rich store of talents you possess,
each one unique, for we are not confined
creations, near snuffed out by circumstance.

You're gifted with a spark – so blow on it
and let it grow in strength to light the world.

# Migration

A flutter caught my eye,
a wing,
perhaps the ghost of one
bestirred by sudden chill,
to dissemble flight again,
as I had seen on hazy summer days
of sage and thyme,
when a swarm of butterflies
uprose, as if just one,
a kaleidoscope of colour.
Each one caught the light and spun,
then drifted skywards,
out of sight.
Migration had begun.

The glory of the moment brought to mind
Christ's time on earth,
a glimpse of heaven.
Disciples, too, were overawed,
but then, as now,
the image was denied by other urgencies,
the frailty of man,
and the brief time was gone.
or so it seemed, once the spirit passed.

Yet here, as then,
a whispered, subtle breath began
to resurrect the memory
and make it live again.
Though the body's withered,
the spirit it contains
seems animate,
yearning for migration, as do we,
to join the host,
the heavenly host,
on wings of butterflies.

# The Tap Dancer

The wheels of thought go round and round –
a tap dance into heaven!

Clack, clackety clack!

The whirring in my brain becomes
a tap dance into heaven,
for my dream is driven by steam!

The whirring in my brain becomes
a train of chugging thought
for my dream is driven by steam!

My mind's
a train of chugging thought
when all of a sudden – it hits a tunnel.

My mind's
going blankety-blank
when, all of a sudden, it hits a tunnel
where my heart skip-hops and stops
going blankety-blank.

I've arrived in tap-dance heaven
where my heart skip-hops and stops.

Dear angel! When you dance with me,
I've arrived in tap dance heaven!
Clack, clackety clack!

Dear angel! When you dance with me…

the wheels of thought…go…round…and…round.

Hmmm!
You lucky devil!

# The Dandelion

I am lost in *Taraxacum*
A foreign land that has become
A new small world to touch and hold,
beloved by bees –
but pollen makes me sneeze!
I love this precious plant of gold.

My dandelion is good to eat –
roots, leaves and flowers – none too sweet.
Its coffee root's a diuret-
ic (absurd word!)
Or 'piss-a-bed', I've heard
while surfing on the internet.

*Dent-de-lion*'s its other name,
straight from the French, or so they claim.
Gallic cuisine this weed esteems.
Its jagged leaf
is like a lion's teeth,
and adds a bite to salad greens.

The flower heads plucked – and this is true –
will make a most delicious brew.
Add boiling water then you've got –
amazingly –
antidepressant tea.
(Ferment them for a wine of sorts.)

Aw, shucks! There can't be more to know,
but what's this stickiness below?
I understand that it's latex –
rubber to you –
farmed for making tyres, too!
This little flower's quite complex!

And now I think it's time to leave
*Taraxacum*, which I believe
is taxonomic jargon for
a weed that's wee'd –
a piss-a-bed indeed!
Goodnight now, folks! It's time to snore.

# Stained Glass

The glass is stained. I see that now
the sun is low, Christ's blood is spilt
across the nave to splash upon
the chaplain's cope, in Easter white.

The sun is low. Christ's blood is spilt,
when guilt upsets his steady hand
the chaplain copes – in Easter white,
he seems so pure, and innocent.

When guilt upsets his steady hand,
he spills the wine. Perhaps unnerved –
he seems so. Pure and innocent,
the choirboys sing the *Agnus Dei*.

He spills the wine. Perhaps unnerved?
The cup replenished now with blood,
the choir boys sing the *Agnus Dei* –
God, forgive us – as he tenders

the cup, replenished now with blood.
The tears that music weeps well out,
God forgive us, as he tenders
a boy, whose treble falters low.

The tears that music weeps, well out
across the nave, to splash upon
this boy, whose treble falters low.
The glass is stained. I see that now.

# The Making of a Poem

Each word has its place,
each place, its meaning,
each meaning, its interpretation,
and thus the poem is born.

In this soft silence,
echoes haunt my solitude,
yet I am not alone.

Memories drag me
into a phantom world
the eye holds dear,
a place where shades and tones
surpass the blinding light,

a place where heartbeats measure time
and circadian rhythm.
My mind, a penned ferment
of ideas, cursive at times,
unwinds the spindle
of my being
(as a spider does),
to weave its words
into swaddling clothes
to bind the infant tight.
The poem opens her eyes
uncertainly,

as if to say,
'Where will you take me today?
Will you be kind,
and treat me gently –
even when I scream?'

As yet, I do not know,
for I am only writing,
and not so real as her.

Realities, for a poet,
as for anyone,
are more difficult to handle
than words,
though words are sometimes hard
and, unlike gloves,
cannot be easily withdrawn.

# Neruda

His words flow like liquid in his own language,
a turbulent and raging torrent
to erode rocks,
and cause avalanches
amongst the stone-hearted;

songs with rhythm
sucked
from the oozing blood
of oppression,
to infuse
the pulse of rebellion;

songs intoned in whispers
deep in the muffled snows
of mountainous
dissent;

songs to thaw
rime-encrusted hatred,
dripping from
the brows of the beaten,

and to undermine cupidity
with the voluptuousness of love.

# Hate

I abominate hate
and execrate the hateful
It is anathema
to feel the fire
of rising odium
of the bête noire
the bitterness of gall
the rankling of revenge
all-consuming animosity
the worm that eats away
at happiness
and joy
replacing them with
revulsion
aversion
and disgust
I abominate hate
but rather like lust

# The Snowdrop

A modest flower with drooping head
stands shyly in the cold.
One might miss it in the snow
but for its tracery of veins;
a verdant green,
suggesting vernal flow.

It seems to whisper,
'Spring comes soon,
when modest maids like me
will set their caps
at likely lads,
who flirt
with urgency.'

A nectared kiss,
a moment's bliss
is all it takes
to pollinate,

…but wait!

Persephone
is Hades' bride.
The snowdrop leads her in
at Candlemas,
when flames burn bright,
cremating sin!

Beware of bringing home
this pallid flower's
distress.
She melts all hearts,
but courts
the cold,
the bitter cold
of death.

# Yearning

Mortal in thought yet not so
when wind bends tree
of pencilled ash,
whose leaves would flow,
immortal now.

Rooted, yet not so
when quickening breezes sway,
a finger's touch away
…away…a finger's touch away.

The pulsing, outstretched limbs
would catch this fleeting wind,
and have it penned
but it is free,
and always so.

These leaves would hold it captive,
but wind
must flee
and, in due time,
leaves let go.

# Echoes of Eternity

A shifting moment hovers
between the past and future,
on wings of possibility,

in an olive grove
where Euterpe lay
with lyric flute;

her drawing in of breath
expelled in fading echoes,
with scarce a sigh;

the echoes of eternity,
part held,
and part let fall;

a cup half full,
ambrosial,
till shattered by reality.

Now shards of meaning glint
in clipped, staccato words,
where memory was spilt;

a strange syntax,
grasped in gravitas
and scrawled in solitude;

a bitter olive
soaked in brine
to take the tannin out,

assaulting tastebuds
with faint memories
of a Grecian mountainside

# Physical Maps

Physical maps show
with hachured lines for steep places
where mountains rise, and rivers flow,
and contours swirl
over the voluptuousness of virginal
landmass,
grounded and unsoiled;
precipitous peaks empurpled,
and deep plumbed depths of blue.

No man-made borders here
on the proud body of Mother Earth,
no shibboleths demarcating the misery
of no-go zones,
no arbitrary lines penning places in,
to claim ownership.

There are no boundaries
but those of nature
as when
the undulating land stands firm
against the writhing of the sea.

## Ducks

As light grows dim, my friend, I would disclose
a favoured spot of mine, beside a lake
with hidden depths to quench the dying flame,
so ducks may glide serenely through the stars,

in line astern across the firmament
when homeward bound, to nest amongst the sedge.
They come in pairs, complete with silhouettes,
each painted likeness mirrored upside down.

O, would that we could cast such shadows too!
Mine own is drab, composed of grayling shades,
of pen and ink. How can that capture light?
Yet as I muse, I ask – out loud it seems –

'Has life been good today?' They answer, 'Quack,'
contentedly. There is no more to say.

# Bigotry

How well contained the fire that warms our heart,
in safety of the hearth
when we're at home,

yet, when wildfire spreads,
it is our doom,
an all-consuming passion once it starts.
When hate's released, good witches burn
and wisdom turns to ash.

Forced to flee
the medieval mindset
once again,
it seems we never learn.

Passion in mankind's a fatal flaw,
a flaming brand to wield in art and war.

# A Reverie

For these are honeyed days when droning bees
assail the blue of tiny borage stars,
with busyness scarce loud enough to spoil
the harmony. The sunshine warms my back
and spills its dappled light on ancient slate.
A gentle seaborne breeze begins to sway
the ghosted boughs of slender eucalypts.
A sudden raucous flight of parakeets
is lost amongst the scintillating leaves.
Their evanescent reds and blues and gold
disperse in pools of light and disappear.
A lavandula haze of purpled bracts
gives pause to resting swarms of butterflies
that stretch their amber wings, then close again
in drowsiness. Is paradise so blest?
My reverie's in tune with tinkling bells
of unicorns that dance against the sky,
dependent on a shoot of Wistar's vine
that twists around a sturdy redgum pile,
to shade this idle poet, penned in thought.

# Making Music

A baby grand! One day she'll play
her heart away.
Just now she thumps
with bangs and bumps,

but give her time and she will be
adept. You'll see!
Such joy she'll give
as will outlive

adversity, producing calm
with music's balm,
to soothe the strife
of daily life.

# The Playground

Turn back the clock to erstwhile,
turn back the clock I say
while I live a second childhood
to hold the Fates at bay.

Together we shall spurn the dusk,
sail eastwards back to dawn,
the Western Isles have beckoned me
but I'll not thereto be borne.

While still there's life, there's gladness
and laughter outweighs tears,
so stay the hand of Atropos,
delay her deadly shears.

# The Moth

How soft the wind doth tease tonight,
the moth paused on the pane.
A feathered brush on powdered wing
reflects the moon's domain.

Its latent form, ephemeral,
seems stilled in dark surmise.
There, painted on its wings outspread,
two iridescent eyes

yearn sightlessly to understand
our filtered firmament.
Yet I could open up the latch
before the candle's spent,

and let this dreamer flutter in
to touch reality,
the flame that burns, reducing all
to grey eternity,

but I'll maintain a poet's right
to keep the window closed,
and pen my prisoned thoughts upon
this moonlit moth's repose.

# Freedom

With luck, we'll flee from circumstance
when all we love is gone,

but, even if successful,
ourselves we'll not outrun.

Raw wounds still bleed the essence
of who we really are.

That precious core,
essential,
needs to heal
and scar,

and not be lost
at any cost.

We
may elude
oppression
but it takes much more than that
to break the bonds
that spiders spin
around a victim's heart.

I speak here for all abused,
for all of those who flee,
and all who are
outcast
from society.

Freedom may be sought,
and its semblance sometimes bought,
but without inner peace
and equanimity,
we're never truly balanced,
never fully free.

# Memento Mori

With grimness we personify
life's only clear cut certainty,
a simple snip to cut the skein,
mute the swan and end the pain.

These days, as I prepare to die,
mementos of the past belie
my own belief that life goes on
beyond the grave, within the song.

I do not think he's clad in black,
a sharpened scythe upon his back.
I face him with tranquillity,
because this monster's only me.

## The Bees

The bees had made this house their own
to labour for their queen
and, finding hollows in the walls,
chewed wax to fill between.

They found their entrance through the roof,
a keyhole made by chance,
where glory vine had twisted tin,
and thus began their dance.

In droves they flew to garden blooms
along the plume of scent,
to lavender and borage plants
upon their business bent,

then staggered back, with pollen sacs
a low-slung heavy load
to slow the homeward journey to
their derelict abode,

whose dusty windows filtered light
on mildew and on mould,
a gutterless, decrepit place,
this house that had grown old.

And here they built a miracle,
social interstices,
a harmony of fellowship
a testament to peace.

What labour! What hexagonies!
What citadels they made!
Each precious cup of honeyed gold
cooled by their winged glissade.

They little knew of man's intent
to resurrect this place
to store his worthless chattels in,

the stuff that spoiled his space.

'Is this your work?' the Maker said,
the Maker of the Bee,
'and were you netted with intent,
you whom I made trustee?

'I see your powder, deadly white,
and corpses by the score
in this, the doleful charnel house,
decaying on the floor.

'A few still crawl the windowpane;
I hear their mournful drone.
The deep morass of death still writhes
with those whose dance is done.

'And why, I pray? Was it for fear
that they might sting your pride,
enclosing them in toxic space –
apian genocide?'

I could not look Him in the eye.
I hung my head in shame.
A miniature decision made,
for which I take the blame.

It's just in scale this differs from
the horrors we create
when nations make their fearful choice.
Attack! Exterminate!

# Petrichor

The aroma of stone
sun-blessed after rain
drops clinging to moss –
lichen's lachrymose stain

The scent of renewal
once clouds have passed by
stones, too, show their hearts
with a tear in the eye

It only takes sunshine
to draw from the earth
the aroma of hope
and love's blessèd rebirth

# The Refugee Children

I should be photographing
young children who are laughing
      on sunlit slopes of grass,
with coronets of daisies
as they cavort like crazy,
      but it's not so…alas.

Instead I hear their wailing
behind the barbed wire railing
      of camps for those displaced
by ceaseless brutal bombing,
and there's no way of calming
      the fears these children faced.

and those whose faith's Islamic
will suffer more…that's tragic,
      and fostering despair.
They pray their mums are coping;
naively they are hoping
      the world will turn out fair.

Remember, they are children,
and futures we are thrilled in
      rely on what we do.
I hope that as they grow up,
their breath is used to blow up
      balloons…not me and you.

No matter which God made us,
He'd find it quite outrageous
      to see the way we act.
The milk of human kindness
seems soured now by blindness.
      Say cheese!
              The lens is cracked.

# The Goodnight Kiss

Now is the time to breathe a blessing,
a benison on silken head,
bestowed before she goes to bed;
the merest brush of lips, a kissing
as gentle as a lamb's tail swishing
contentedly, whilst being fed.
There are no sins to be confessing,
the book is closed, the tale is read,
the monster's slain, no more oppressing,
her mother's prayers will keep him dead.
The child is safe with her caressing,
as now with love she breathes her blessing,
a benison on silken head.

# Faith

Let
your light
be subdued
lest it blind me,
Faith

# This is the Deep

This is the deep, the dreadful deep
beyond the pain of red,
where dreams, like plankton,
swirl through weed,
the widow's weeds of dread,
and gently land
to join the dross
upon the sea's dark floor.
Dreams drowned in deed,
or lack of it;
a loss, but lost no more.

# A Pair of Piping Shrikes

Two piping shrikes, birds of magpie hue,
sang their serenade as I went about my work.
You'd think a shrike might pipe
a shrill and wailing skirl,
sending shivers down the back,
but that's not true!

Their song's a throaty ripple,
like the babble of a creek,
a most melodious warble,
a very cheerful gurgle,
that echoes through the garden
from the hay shed roof,

but treat these birds with caution,
diminuendos dropping
on the ears of those who listen,
belie their beady eyes
and sharp, strong beaks,

as in the springtime season,
when chicks are hatched and hungry,
defending territory,
they will often swoop.

Beware the shrieking shrike!
In parental mode
they strike,
and their beaks draw blood
from the likes of me and you!

# Westminster Bridge, 22 March 2017

I fondly recollect a bridge most fair
where William Wordsworth, with his poet's eye,
remarked upon an air of majesty.
Now Londoners, in grief, black armbands wear;
their heads are bowed this day in silence, bare,
to honour innocents who, passing by,
were callously mown down and left to die.
Once more fanaticism sours the air,
its jaundiced mists designed to creep
and cause despair. They call it Allah's will,
but it is not. Our gods must surely weep
to see ascribed to them such grievous ill.
Yet Britons will not let this terror steep
their lives in bile, though mighty hearts lie still.

# The River

Diffuse the light of this half-whispered dawn,
as river mists reveal a hidden pool,
its silver dappled by a sun-blotched fawn
that's come to drink at Styx's vestibule.

Above begins the warbler's soft hoo-eet
as golden rays reveal its drab disguise,
and trailing willow fronds reach down to meet
a sudden plop of water vole! Surprise!

But now the mists have cleared, new day's begun,
and river craft chug by with raucous hoots.
A noisy crowd of yahoos bless the sun
with clumsy splashing. Carefree young galoots

All life enjoys the river's endless song.
Eternity is now, but moves along.

www.ingramcontent.com/pod-product-compliance
Lightning Source LLC
Chambersburg PA
CBHW070101120526
44589CB00033B/1346